Beautiful By Design

Love who you are...We are different but the same!

Copyright

Additional Credits

Illustrator: Dominique Bennett

Front Cover Art: Dominique Bennett

Additional Artwork by: Daniel Ekanayake

Book Designer: Sam George

DEDICATION

Dedicated to all my young ladies whom I have nurtured, mentored and watched flourish over the years, and to all little girls who need to know they are indeed beautiful by design.

Foreword

Christine Bertrand-Clarke

I have always loved books, and developed an appreciation of literature,
during my childhood years. I recently joined a small creative writing group,
which birthed the desire to write a book myself. This little book is my
response to the racial inequalities that I witnessed in the world.

It has a special message of affirmation for young girls of colour, and seeks to
encourage all young readers to appreciate cultural diversity, in a
lighthearted way. It is my hope that parents will use this book as a resource
tool to help their children broaden their perspective of others through
cultural awareness, while they learn to love who they are, as they were
created.

When we learn about each other, we learn to value our differences.

Value our differences
Daniel Ekanayake

God created me in his image.

We look different, but we are the same.

All created as individuals.

He knew us before we came.

All of us

We were born unique.

Being different isn't so bad.

I don't look like you, I am not the same.

I am special too, that makes me glad.

Your skin is light and very fair.

While mine is dark in shade.

This is who I am, and I look good too.

I am fearfully and wonderfully made!

Your eyes are coloured an azure blue.

While mine are pigmented brown.

I think God was just having fun, spreading creativity around!

Your hair is blonde, with the texture straight.

While I have black, with tight swirls.

God wrapped mine around his fingers.

And gave me a full head of curls.

Though we look different on the outside.

Inside we are all the same.

When I am unhappy, I cry just like you.

When I am hurt, I too feel pain.

We all have different traditions.

Culture is a part of who we are.

From what we eat, to what we wear.

Customs have followed us from afar.

God created us just as HE wanted.

You don't have to feel so afraid.

Yes I am not like you. I LOVE who I am.

For I am fearfully and wonderfully made!

So let's learn about each other.

Your life matters and so does mine.

Each of us has great value.

Created "Beautiful by Design!"

About The Author

Christine Bertrand-Clarke was born on the island of Jamaica, and raised and educated in England. She is a professional Nurse currently working and living in Canada. Christine is a devoted Christian, wife and mother, and a self-professed crafting queen. Christine is an avid reader and loves books with positive and uplifting messages. "Beautiful by Design" is her first publication for children.

About the Illustrator

17 year-old Dominique Bennett is a high school student with a passion for art!

She is inspired by anime,manga and video game art and creates her original line art characters.

She has her own clothing line under DSB Designz.

Dominique is thrilled to have her illustrations published for the first time in this premiere work by Christine Bertrand-Clarke.

Acknowledgement

I wish to sincerely thank all who shared in the unfolding of this little book. Thank God our Father for his continual grace, mercy, presence and direction in my life. He is faithful.

Special thank you to my husband Mike and my son Alexander for their love and support.

The Lakeside Church (TLC), our Community and Extended family. The TLC Creative Writing Team. Thank you all for your guidance, ideas, and input and for sharing the literary journey.